The Italians

Kathleen Fahey

CRABTREE
Publishing Company
www.crabtreebooks.com

CRABTREE
Publishing Company

PMB 16A 350 Fifth Avenue
Suite 3308
New York, NY 10118

612 Welland Avenue
St. Catharines, Ontario
L2M 5V6

Co-ordinating editor: Ellen Rodger
Content editor: Virginia Mainprize
Consulting editor: Lisa Gurusinghe
Production co-ordinator: Rosie Gowsell
Cover design: Robert MacGregor

Film: Embassy Graphics

Printer: Worzalla Publishing Company

Created by: Brown Partworks Ltd
Commissioning editor: Anne O'Daly
Project editor: Caroline Beattie
Picture researcher: Adrian Bentley
Editorial assistant: Chris Wiegand
Maps: Mark Walker
Consultant: Professor Donald Avery

CATALOGING-IN-PUBLICATION DATA
Fahey, Kathleen, 1961-
    The Italians / Kathleen Fahey.–1st ed.
      p.cm. – (We came to North America)
    Includes index.
    ISBN 0-7787-0189-1 (RLB) – ISBN 0-7787-0203-0 (pbk.)
    1. Italian Americans–History–Juvenile literature.
2. Italian Americans–Biography–Juvenile literature. [1. Italian Americans.] I. Title. II. Series.
    E184.I8 F25 2001
    973'.0451–dc21
                        00-034607
                        LC

Photographs
The Art Archive 8, 17 (top), back cover; Brown Partworks Library of Congress 16 (top), 18, 23 (top); Corbis, 17 (bottom); National Archives 10; Canadian Broadcasting Corporation 31 (bottom); Peter Crabtree 5 (bottom), 7 (top); David H. Wells 19; Kelly-Mooney Photography 25 (top); Michael S. Yamashita 28; Robert Holmes 29 (bottom); Wolfgang Kaehler 5 (top); Glenbow Archives, Calgary, Canada (NA-5596-5) front cover, 25 (bottom), (NA-5124-9) 29 (top); Hulton Getty 15 (top); The Image Bank Archive Photos 7 (bottom), 9 (bottom), 11 (bottom). Mary Evans Picture Library 6 (top), 17 (bottom); North Wind Picture Archives 14, 21; Peter Newark's Pictures 9 (top), 11 (top), 13, 16 (bottom), 23 (bottom), 27, 30 (bottom), 31 (top); Ronald Grant Archive 30 (top); Tony Stone Images Laurie Evans 24.

Special thanks to Lisa Antonsen and the Schiralli family for the family photo that appears on page 19 (top).

Cover: An Italian-American celebrates Columbus Day, the holiday that marks Christopher Columbus' arrival in America.

Book Credits
page 12: *Ellis Island: Echoes from a Nation's Past,* Susan Jonas ed., published by Aperture in association with the National Park Service, U.S. Department of the Interior, and Montclair State College.

page 20: *Scorsese on Scorsese,* David Thompson and Ian Christie eds., published by Faber and Faber Ltd, 1989.

page 26: *Rosa: The Life of an Italian Immigrant* by Marie Hall Ets, © 1970. The University of Minnesota.

Contents

Introduction

▲ An early drawing shows Native Americans meeting Amerigo Vespucci and his crew as they arrive in South America.

The first Italians came to North and South America over 500 years ago. An Italian sailor, Christopher Columbus, reached North America in 1492. The Queen of Spain had sent him to sail west across the Atlantic Ocean and find a new trade route to China and Japan. He landed on an island in the Caribbean and thought he had reached Asia. Italian explorer, Amerigo Vespucci, gave his name to the Americas. He went to South America in 1499, and a mapmaker later named the area "America" in his honor.

John Cabot was another famous Italian explorer. He lived most of his life in Venice, a city in Italy. When he was 46, he moved to England and changed his name from Giovanni Caboto to John Cabot. In 1497, he was sent by the King of England to search for a sea route to Asia. Instead, he reached a huge island off the east coast of Canada. He called it "New Founde Landes" and claimed it for England. Today, the island is a province of Canada, called Newfoundland.

Since then, millions of Italians have come to North America. The first **immigrants** were from northern Italy and arrived after the 1820s. Many of these Italians settled in California. Some grew grapes and opened **wineries**. Others planted fruit orchards and vegetable farms. Some of these businesses became large and successful.

Most Italians arrived in the United States and Canada in the late 1800s. They left the hardship and poverty of their home villages, looking for a better life in "Lamerica," as they called North America. Most of them came with few skills and little money. They hoped to find opportunities they did not have in Italy. Often, their dreams of a better future came true, if not for themselves, at least for their children and grandchildren.

During the last 120 years, Italian Americans and Italian Canadians have worked hard, educated their children, and have become valuable citizens. Some have succeeded in government, in music and the arts, and in sports. Others have made contributions to science and business.

▲ **The Cabot Tower in Newfoundland marks Cabot's landing there in 1497.**

Times of Trouble

About 2000 years ago, Italy was the center of one of the great and powerful Roman Empire. Romans were great scholars, engineers, and artists. Many of their great works of art are in museums. After the defeat of the Romans by fierce tribes, Italy was a divided land for centuries. Some parts were ruled by kings and queens from other countries, and others by local princes. Italians often rebelled against their rulers, but it was not until 1871 that Italy became a united country with its own king. However, life was still hard, especially in the south. To escape these times of trouble, many Italians left their homeland, looking for a better life in North America.

▲ **The Romans were great artists and sculptors. This bust copies the style of the Greeks.**

Flight from Poverty

In the late 1800s, life was hard for most people in southern Italy. The country was going through a time of political troubles, and crop failures had caused widespread starvation.

Most of the Italians who came to the United States and Canada in the late 1800s were from southern Italy. At that time, the north was becoming **industrialized**, and people there were getting jobs in factories and offices. The south was still mostly farmland owned by rich landowners who often lived far from their properties. They rented the land to farmers who were charged so much rent that they made little profit after selling their extra crops. Taxes were also high, and some farmers, who could not afford to pay them, were driven off their land. Years of dry weather and a disease which destroyed many of the **vineyards** left many peasant farmers, or *contadini*, impoverished.

Other workers, such as carpenters and stone cutters, could not find enough work to support their families. The only hope for many desperate Italians was to leave the villages where their families had lived for hundreds of years and to move to another country.

▲ Some Italians did not have enough money to feed themselves and their families. They were forced to beg from rich people.

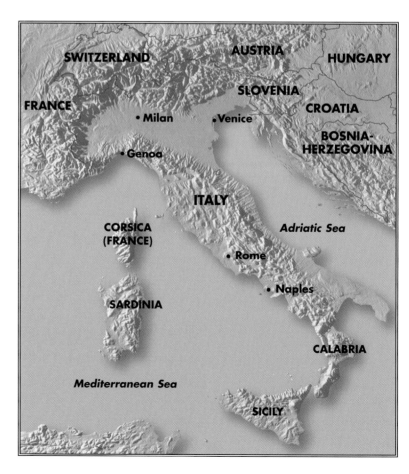

▶Most Italians who immigrated to North America left from the south of Italy.

Vineyard Disaster

One of Italy's most important businesses in the late 1800s and today is winemaking. Grapes, which grow well on the sunny slopes, are pressed into juice that is allowed to **ferment** into wine. In the late nineteenth century, plant **lice** attacked thousands of Italian vineyards, destroying the grape vines. At the same time, France began charging high taxes on **imported** Italian wines to protect its own wine industry. Italian wines became too expensive for most French people to buy. The Italian wine industry suffered, and many farmers could not find a market for their grapes. Laborers, who were usually hired by the owners of large vineyards, could not find work.

▲ **Grapes and olives were the two most important crops of southern Italy.**

Some Italians went to other parts of Europe. However, most of the people who left Italy in the late 1800s traveled to North America. The invention of the steamship had made the journey across the Atlantic shorter, less dangerous, and much less expensive than it had been in the past. For many Italians, North America was known as the land of opportunity where everyone had a chance to get rich. They believed that, even if they did not become millionaires, they could find jobs, support their families, and educate their children.

▶ **Southern Italians did not own their farms. They paid high rent to their landlords.**

The Journey

In the 1880s, the journey from Italy to North America took two to four weeks by steamship, depending on the weather and the route. Passengers traveled on one of three classes: first class, for passengers who could afford the ticket; second class, which was less expensive, and third class, the least comfortable and the cheapest.

Because even a third-class ticket was so expensive for Italian farmers, the first immigrants from Italy in the 1880s were usually men traveling alone. Most of them were single and young. Others were married men leaving their wives and families behind them. They hoped to make enough money either to return home rich or to send for their families to join them. Later, entire families made the journey to North America.

These immigrants traveled third class, or steerage, deep in the hold, or bottom, of the ship. Conditions were uncomfortable and crowded.

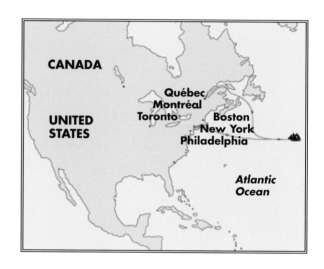

▲ Most Italians who immigrated to North America first settled in eastern cities.

◄ Italians wait on the dock, ready to board their steamship. They carry only a few possessions, in baskets, suitcases, or wrapped in bundles.

Not an Easy Life

Italian immigrants left their country filled with hope for a better life. Visitors, returning to Italy from North America, had told them how good life was in the United States and Canada and how easy it was to get a high-paying job. These visitors wore their best clothes and carried plenty of money in their pockets. In comparison with the people in the poor villages of southern Italy, they seemed to be rich and successful. However, life was hard for many Italians who had moved to North America, but they were too proud to admit it.

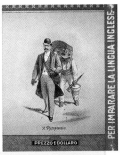

▲ This "emigrants' book" shows a man leaving his home and family in Italy. The next page shows him returning as a rich man.

▼ Hundreds of immigrants were crowded together in the hold of ships that traveled to North America.

Third-class passengers slept on narrow bunk beds, stacked three high. There was no fresh air, few toilets, no showers, and no place to wash clothes. In these unhealthy conditions, disease spread easily. Some immigrants became sick, and, without proper medical treatment, some died before they reached North America. Third-class passengers were often not fed on the ship and had to bring their own food. If the steamship company provided food, it was brought down from the kitchens in huge pails. When the sea was rough, many people got so seasick they couldn't eat. The only way to escape the foul-smelling air was to come up on the steerage deck.

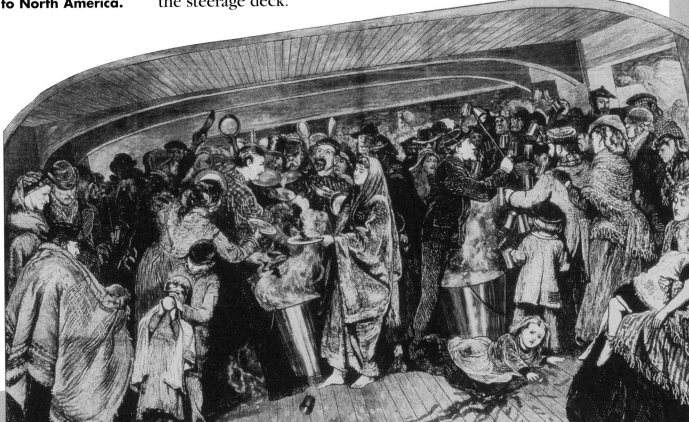

First Impressions

After spending weeks in a crowded hold, it was a relief for immigrants to see land. However, their journey was not over yet. They still had to pass tests before being allowed into North America.

After their long, hard voyage, immigrants were happy finally to arrive at their **destination**, but they were also worried about their future. They were moving to a new country with different customs and another language. Most of them were bringing little money with them and had no place to live. They also knew they would be questioned and checked before they were allowed to land. If they failed the tests, they could be sent back to Italy.

Most Italians who came to the United States after 1892 were taken to the immigration station on Ellis Island in the bay outside New York City. First- and second-class passengers were allowed to land first. Third-class passengers often had to wait on board ship for days until they were herded onto overcrowded barges and taken to the immigration center.

▲ Ellis Island is in the bay just off New York City. Immigrants knew that if they failed their tests there, they would be sent home.

Crooks and Thieves

Most of the immigrants who arrived at Ellis Island did not speak English. People of all ages arrived tired, confused, and hungry. Most of them had little money. They were often treated rudely and unfairly. Immigration officers sometimes asked for bribes to speed up the process. Moneychangers tried to cheat immigrants, and railroad agents sometimes overcharged them for train tickets.

Immigrants were taken to a huge inspection hall, about the size of a football field. They had to stand in long lines, waiting to be checked. Two doctors examined each immigrant: one, for physical and mental fitness, the other, for signs of disease. If doctors saw any sign of sickness, they made a chalk mark on the person's right shoulder. People with chalk marks were separated from their friends and families and were sent for a closer medical examination.

After passing the medical exam, each immigrant was asked 29 questions by an **interpreter**. Some of the questions were: What kind of work do you do? Where are you going? How much money do you have? Have you ever been in prison? Some immigrants were so frightened and confused they had trouble answering the questions. Most people passed the test and were allowed to enter the United States. At last, they were on their way to a new life.

In Canada, most immigrants passed through Grosse-Ile, the immigration station for the port of Québec from 1832-1937. Although it had been the site of terrible **epidemics** in the past, by the late 1800s Grosse Ile was well run. After leaving Grosse Ile, Italians traveled by train to their destinations, usually a large city, such as Montréal or Toronto.

▲ **Cheap railroad tickets helped new immigrants travel to the west coast.**

▶ **Immigrants go on to a new life after passing their tests at Ellis Island.**

Eyewitness to History

ROCCO MORELLI was twelve when he arrived at Ellis Island in 1907. He describes what happened when he arrived there.

 We were on Ellis Island 22 days. They took all us men to one section of the room, and they stripped us. They took all our clothes and they only left our papers in our hands. We went through something like a cattle booth. At all of these booths there was a doctor who examined you. If you were a sick person they told you to wait. If you were all right you continued with the rest of the examination. They looked at your whole body — the eyes, the heart, the teeth. They brought us into a big hall. All of a sudden they called your name and your clothes appeared. All clean and packed and smelling nice, because, to tell the truth, I've got to be honest about it, they **deloused** us. As I said, the ship we came over on wasn't a clean ship. You couldn't clean yourself anyway because even the water from the fountains was frozen. In order to drink some water we had to break the ice with something and melt it. So how can you keep yourself clean?

False Promises

In the 1880s, North American cities were growing fast. Workers were needed in factories, in the construction business, and to build the railroads. Companies paid Italians living in North America to go to Italy and find people to come and work in Canada and the United States. These agents were called *padroni* in Italian.

Many of the farmers in the villages of southern Italy had never even heard of Canada and the United States. *Padroni* came to their villages and told stories about the land of opportunity across the ocean. They promised people good jobs. Most Italians did not have enough money to buy steamship tickets to North America for themselves and their families. *Padroni* lent people who wanted to leave Italy the money for the journey. In return, they promised to repay the *padroni*. After arriving in North America, immigrants discovered they had to give a large part of their salary to the *padroni* each month. They had to pay back the money they had been lent along with a high rate of **interest**. Since many Italians worked at low-paying jobs, they found themselves in debt for many years. Many dishonest *padroni* became rich by **exploiting** immigrant workers in this way.

▶ Children were treated like slaves by the *padroni*. This boy is being trained as a ragpicker.

The Foran Act

Padroni forced immigrants to work for little pay. Companies were eager to hire Italian workers because they accepted such low wages. Other workers were angry because they could not compete with the Italians. Labor unions, such as the Order of the Knights of Labor, pressured the U.S. government to protect jobs from competition from immigrants. In 1885, Congress passed the Foran Act, making it illegal to import workers into the United States. Companies who brought in workers from other countries had to pay fines. However, there were no inspectors to check if employers were obeying the law.

▲ **The leaders of the Order of the Knights of Labor in 1886.**

At first, *padroni* brought mostly children from poor southern Italian families to work in North America as acrobats, shoeshiners, and musicians. They were forced to work long hours, were underfed, and had to give all the money they earned to the *padroni*. These children were treated so badly that in the 1880s the Italian government made it illegal for *padroni* to get children in Italy. Instead, *padroni* began finding adults to come and work in North America. Many of these unskilled and uneducated workers ended up in debt to the *padroni* for years. By 1897, these agents controlled most of the Italian laborers who worked in the construction business in New York City.

After a while, the *padroni* lost their power, and their role in the Italian community changed. They became employment agents, finding jobs for new arrivals and being interpreters for them until they learned to understand and speak English. *Padroni* still took advantage of immigrants, charging them a high fee to help them find work. However, as soon as they could find work on their own, Italians turned away from the *padroni*.

◀ **Children were put to work for long hours by their *padroni*. These tired-looking girls are selling baskets at night.**

15

Finding Work

Although most Italians had been farmers in Italy, when they came to North America they settled in cities. Many stayed in New York City, the port where most Italians arrived. Others went to Boston, Chicago, and Philadelphia, and, in Canada, to Montréal and Toronto.

Most of the new immigrants from southern Italy had no job training and little education. Usually, they could not read and write. They often had trouble finding work and were glad to take any job they could get. Many of the new arrivals found low-paying work with construction and railway companies or on the docks. In New York, three-quarters of the laborers in the construction business were Italian. Many of these workers built the New York subway.

Other immigrants found jobs in factories. In Italy, most women stayed at home, looking after the house, raising large families, and helping with the farm work. In the United States and Canada, women flooded the work force. Many worked in the garment industry, in factories making clothes for the rapidly growing population.

▲ Italian families with many children were hired to pick cranberries.

▼ Italian fishers in San Francisco in 1910.

▲ Some Italians went to work in stone quarries.

Some Italians crossed the continent and settled in California and British Columbia. They worked in vineyards and orchards and on farms as they had in Italy. Because banks did not want to lend money to immigrant farmers, an Italian American, Amadeo Peter Giannini, opened a bank where Italian immigrants could borrow money to buy their own land. Some of these hard-working farmers prospered. Other Italians, especially those from Sicily, worked in the fish industry on the west coast.

Many Italians were brought to Pennsylvania in the 1890s to work in the marble and granite **quarries**, digging and cutting stone. Italians also helped build the railways in North America or worked in mines and steel mills. Some saved their money and opened small stores, selling fruit and vegetables and groceries.

Men, women, and children worked long, hard days for low pay. Some Italians did not find life in North America as they had imagined. Nearly half of the Italian immigrants who came to the United States and Canada between 1876 and 1924 returned home.

A Success Story

When Amadeo Obici was just eleven years old, he left his small village in Italy to seek his fortune in the United States. He arrived in New York in 1887, speaking no English. His first job was in a hotel, as a bellhop carrying guests' suitcases. Later, he opened his own fruit stand. With his savings, he bought a peanut roaster and a horse and wagon and became a peanut **vendor**. This business grew, and in 1906, Amadeo founded Planters Peanuts. At first, the company was small, with six workers and two large roasters. After Amadeo married Louise Musate, who operated her own peanut stand in Wilkes-Barre, Pennsylvania, the couple opened a factory in Virginia. Planters Peanuts grew, and the Obicis became rich. They never forgot their family and friends and became generous **benefactors** of their community

◄ Mr. Peanut, the mascot for Planter's Peanuts. The company was started by Amadeo Obici.

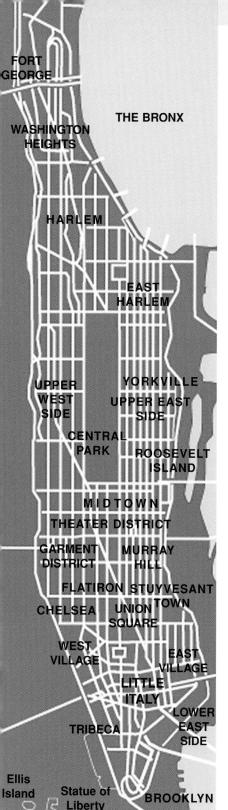

Little Italies

Italian immigrants usually moved into the part of the city where other Italians lived and where they had friends and relatives. These districts became known as "Little Italies."

Little Italies grew up in many North American cities, including New York City, Boston, and Toronto. In some of these neighborhoods, the Italian population was so large that immigrants from the same village in Italy settled on the same streets. Here they could speak their own Italian dialect, eat Italian food, hear Italian music, go to their own church, and celebrate their own holidays. They could find help and support from family and friends.

Many Little Italies were in the oldest and most rundown areas where rents were cheap. Living conditions were bad. Large families were crowded into small rooms in apartment houses called tenements. Many apartments had no running water, and families shared a tap in the hallway. Some families even lived in dark, damp cellars. People were overworked, and sometimes they did not get enough food. Disease spread easily, and death rates were often much higher than in other parts of the city.

▲ **New York's Little Italy is in the south of the city.**

▶ **An immigrant mother at home with her baby.**

18

▲ Italians from New York, visiting their relatives in Toronto's Little Italy in 1946.

Over the years, as they became more successful and had more money, many Italians moved out of their Little Italies. However, these communities have survived. New York City, Boston, and Toronto have Little Italies that are thriving business centers where traditional festivals are still celebrated. Even people who have no Italian background love to come to these neighborhoods to buy Italians specialties and eat in Italian restaurants.

Mutual Aid Societies

Italians had a tradition of hard work, of being careful with money, and strong family ties. They did not like to accept charity from the government when they fell on hard times. They preferred to help each other. Italians in the U.S. and Canada formed mutual aid societies to help new immigrants find housing and work. When jobs were scarce and many people had trouble supporting themselves and their families, these societies helped members of the community. Today, they still support Italian North Americans, offering college scholarships to students who cannot afford to pay for their education. They also sponsor cultural centers where Italian Americans and Italian Canadians can go to meet each other and share their traditions.

▼ The Order of the Sons of Italy in the U.S. prepare for a parade.

ORDER SONS OF ITALY IN AMERICA

PROGRESO LODGE 1147 SYRACUSE N.Y.

Eyewitness to History

MARTIN SCORSESE, the film director, was born in New York in 1942. His grandparents were Italian immigrants from Sicily who came to the United States around 1910. Here, he tells of his upbringing in New York's Little Italy.

" My parents were born on Elizabeth Street, in the Lower East Side of Manhattan, and worked in the garment district. But until I was seven or eight years old we lived in a place called Corona in the suburb of Queens…. Then my father ran into business problems and we had to move back to a tenement building on the block where he was born. We stayed for four or five months with my grandparents until we could find some other rooms, and this was a terrifying experience because I was old enough to realize that there were some tough guys around…

At this time the Italian American community lived in a series of about ten blocks, starting from Houston Street down to Chinatown at Canal Street. The three main blocks were on Elizabeth Street, Mott Street and Mulberry Street. Little Italy was very sharply defined, so often the people from one block wouldn't hang out with those from another. Elizabeth Street was mainly Sicilian, as were my grandparents, and here the people had their own regulations and laws. "

Wartime

The 1920s were a time of change in Italy. Benito Mussolini and his followers, known as the fascists, took over the government.

Enlist in the NAVY

When Mussolini became **dictator**, many Italians in North America thought he would do good things for Italy. They believed that his strong government would make the country richer and more powerful, and they supported the fascists. Many other Canadians and Americans, who disapproved of Mussolini's government because it was not **democratic**, became hostile to Italians living in North America.

In 1940, Mussolini involved Italy in World War II on the side of Germany and Japan, the enemies of the United States and Canada. This move shocked Italian North Americans. They withdrew their support for Mussolini and his government.

▲ A military recruiting poster aimed at all the different immigrant groups in the United States.

Even so, the U.S. and Canadian governments were worried that some Italian North Americans would take sides with Italy against them. They feared that Italian Americans living on the coast might help enemy ships. Italian-American fishers had their boats taken from them. They could no longer support themselves and their families. About 1600 Italian Americans were put into **internment** camps. Because thousands of Italian Americans were forbidden to travel, many lost their jobs. These people and their families suffered many hardships.

In Canada, all Italian Canadians were forced to register with the police. Hundreds of men were put into an internment camp in Ontario because the government feared they might support the fascists. Italian shops were **broken into** and looted. To avoid this **discrimination**, some Italians changed their names to make them sound more English.

Despite this treatment, over 500,000 Italian Americans and Canadians joined their countries' armed services. Many were part of the forces sent to free Italy towards the end of the war.

▶ **Italian Americans in New York watch as a flag is raised in honor of neighborhood men at war.**

Liberating Italy

Over 500,000 Italian Americans and Canadians joined their countries' armed services in World War II. Some fought in the armies that freed Italy towards the end of the war. After landing in southern Italy in 1943, the **Allies** marched north. They met little resistance from the Italian army, and eventually the Italian government surrendered. However, German troops, which had occupied Italy, continued to fight hard. They tried desperately to keep the allied armies from advancing. Little by little, the allies pushed the German forces north. Rome fell to the allies in 1944, and by 1945 Germany was defeated. Many more Italians emigrated to North America in the 1950s when Italy was stilll recovering from the effects of the war. Many of these later Italian immigrants settled in cities and found work in the construction industry, building houses, skyscrapers, and roads.

Language, Food, and Music

The Italians who came to North America brought their language, customs, and music with them. Many of these traditions have been kept alive in churches, family celebrations, and community events.

In Italy, each region had its own customs and food. Even the language could change from one region to another, with people speaking different dialects of Italian. In North America, Italian immigrants began speaking a mixture of their local language and English. Many English words became Italianized. For example, "boss" became "bosso" and "job" became "giobba." Speaking this mixed language made it easier for people from different regions of Italy to understand each other.

When North Americans think of Italian food, they usually think of pizza and spaghetti. However, Italian cooking is much more varied. Each region of Italy has its own specialties and cooking style, depending on the local ingredients that are available.

Pizza Comes to North America

Pizza was originally a dish from Naples, a city in southern Italy. Made of bread dough topped with tomatoes, herbs, and cheese, it was baked in a stone oven. In 1905, Gennaro Lombardi, an Italian restaurant owner in New York's Little Italy began to serve pizza to his customers. It reminded them of home. Today, pizza is one of North America's most popular foods. Pizzeria's can be found in almost any city or town.

▲ **Some of the food and drink that many North Americans enjoy today, such as pizza, and a type of strong coffee, called espresso, were brought by Italians.**

A basic part of the diet of the first Italian immigrants was coarse black bread. They also ate vegetables, such as tomatoes, onions, corn, and peas. Pasta, such as spaghetti, was a luxury in Italy. Most people could afford to eat it only once or twice a year, on special occasions. In North America, although immigrants still had little money, they could eat pasta two or three times a week. Pasta became a staple food of the Italian North American diet.

Italian food was unknown in North America before the arrival of the Italian immigrants. Today, Italian food is enjoyed in many homes, restaurants, and fast-food outlets across the continent.

Music is an important part of Italian life and is enjoyed at special occasions, holidays, and family celebrations, such as weddings. Violin, mandolin, and accordion music were especially popular among Italian immigrants who sometimes brought their musical instruments with them. Opera, an Italian musical tradition in which a story is sung by singers taking different roles, is popular with Italians and many other North Americans.

▲ Although some Italian North Americans no longer speak Italian, they are proud of their heritage.

▼ Italian-Canadian children perform dances brought over from Italy.

Eyewitness to History

ROSA CASSETTARI came to the United States at the end of the nineteenth century. Here, Rosa shows how important it was for immigrants to learn to speak English.

"I was shaking and shivering when we came out in the station, but I just smiled at Lorenzo and marched up to the man at the gate: 'Please will you tell me where to get the train to New York?'

'The train to New York? In one hour it goes.' The officer held up one finger and took out his watch and showed me. Then he motioned to one of the long seats. 'You sit down and wait there and I will tell you when it is time.'

'Thank you, *signore*. Thank you.'

Think of that! I had talked English to a strange man and he had understood me. Lorenzo was looking at me like I was something wonderful. So then I started watching the clock and counting the minutes. But that minute hand moved so slow that I thought the clock must be wrong. So I went back to the man by the gate — I wasn't afraid at all. In America the poor can talk to anyone and ask what they want to know. "

Religion and Traditions

Italians immigrating to North America brought their religious traditions with them. They practiced Roman Catholicism, the Christian religion of most Italians for many centuries.

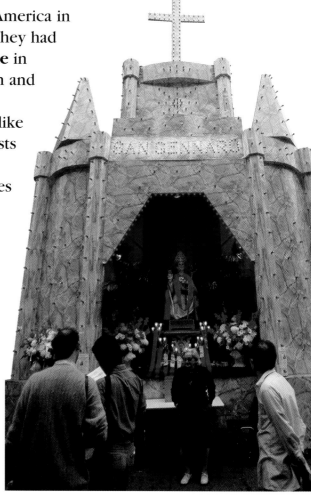

▼ A shrine in honor of San Gennaro in New York's Little Italy. It has been decorated for the feast of San Gennaro.

In Italy, each region had its own **patron saint**, whom Catholics prayed to and honored. Each saint's feast day was celebrated by a special festival, called a *feste*. Festes were noisy and happy occasions with a parade in which people carried the saint's statue through the streets.

When Italian immigrants began coming to North America in the 1880s, the largest Catholic group was the Irish. They had begun to arrive in the 1840s, after the terrible **famine** in Ireland. At first, Italians had no churches of their own and had to go to Irish churches. Because Italian religious customs were different from theirs, the Irish did not like the Italians coming to their services. Some Irish priests did not allow Italians to come to their church. Sometimes, they made Italians attend religious services in the basement, separate from the rest of the **congregation**. They discouraged Italians from celebrating their own religious festivals to honor their patron saints.

As their population grew, Italians began building their own churches. These buildings became places where they could worship in their own way. They were also centers where Italians could meet, help each other, and share their traditions. Italian priests and nuns were sent from Italy to work with the Italian immigrants. They set up Catholic schools where Italian children could learn about their religion and culture.

Over the years, as the immigrants' children grew up and had their own children, religion and the church became less important in Italian communities. This change often caused conflict between the different generations in Italian families. Although most Italian North Americans are still Catholic, religion today plays a less central role in their life. Religious events, such as **baptisms** and weddings, are still important family occasions.

▲ An Italian-Canadian family celebrates a baptism in Alberta in 1927.

An Italian-American Saint

Mother Frances Cabrini was a Roman Catholic nun. She was sent by the pope, the leader of the Catholic Church from Italy to the United States in 1889 to work with the many Italian immigrants who needed help. Soon after she arrived in New York, she started an orphanage, or home for Italian children whose parents had died or could not look after them. With a group of other nuns, she set up hospitals and schools for children of Italian background. The Roman Catholic Church named Mother Cabrini America's first saint in 1946.

▲ Mother Cabrini was made a saint.

Here to Stay

Italian North-Americans have made great contributions to their communities and their countries. Here are a few short biographies of Italian Americans and Italian Canadians who have been successful in their fields.

Many first-generation Italians could not read or write, but they knew the importance of a good education. Many of their descendants have achieved the success their immigrant grandparents and parents dreamed about for their children. Some have college and university degrees. Others are successful and respected doctors, lawyers, scientists, and teachers.

▲ Francis Ford Coppola at work during the filming of *The Godfather Part III.*

Filmmaker, Francis Ford Coppola, was born in Detroit, Michigan, in 1939. After college, he directed his first feature film. His later movie about an Italian-American **Mafia** family, *The Godfather* (1972), was a huge box-office success. It is considered a masterpiece. His other famous movies include *The Godfather Part II* and *Apocalypse Now*, about the Vietnam War. He runs his own film production company and is one of the most-respected movie directors today.

Madonna Ciccone, actress and pop star, was born in a suburb of Detroit. She acted and danced as a child. Later, she moved to New York to follow a musical career. After recording several hit songs, she began appearing in movies. Her **controversial** shows and her talent in knowing what her fans want have made her one of the world's richest and most successful stars.

◄ Joe DiMaggio, the Italian-American baseball player, is pictured on the left with teammate Mickey Mantle. Joe DiMaggio was possibly the best all-round player of his time. He won the Most Valuable Player Award three times.

Frank Sinatra Did it His Way

Frank Sinatra, the son of Italian immigrants was born in the Italian section of Hoboken, New Jersey. Brought up in a family that loved music, Frank began to sing professionally with local clubs while he was still in high school. In 1942, he decided to go solo. Touring the country, singing on two radio shows and starring in his first movie, Frank soon became known as "The Voice". Millions of people fell in love with his deep voice singing romantic songs. Frank Sinatra also had an Oscar-winning movie career. Although he died in 1998, his recordings are still popular around the world.

◀ **Late in his career, Frank Sinatra recorded his signature song "My Way."**

▼ **The Italian-Canadian actor Bruno Gerussi starred in the popular television series *The Beachcombers*. It ran for eighteen years.**

Antonin Scalia, the Italian-American Supreme Court judge, was born in Trenton, New Jersey, in 1936. His father was an immigrant from Sicily. Scalia graduated at the top of his class from Georgetown University and later from Harvard Law School. President Ronald Reagan nominated him a Supreme Court Justice.

The Italian-Canadian painter, Guido Molinari, was born in Montréal. He was a leader in **abstract** painting, and his work features the use of narrow bands or wide stripes. Molinari's work is recognized in Europe as well as North America.

Sam Grana, the filmmaker and actor, was born in Italy and immigrated to Canada with his family when he was six years old. He helped to develop the "alternative drama" film that is used in many documentaries. Many of Grana's films are about the life and times of Italian-Canadians.

Glossary

Allies A group of countries that fought together against Germany in WW II.

abstract A style of painting that is not realistic.

baptism A Christian ceremony representing spiritual re-birth.

benefactors Someone who gives aid or assistance.

congregation Members of a religious group who meet regularly.

controversial Something that causes an argument between to groups of people.

deloused Treated in order to get rid of lice (biting insects) from a person's body, hair, and clothing.

democratic Government by the people.

destination A place where one is going.

dialect A regional variety of a language.

dictator A ruler who listens to no one. A tyrant.

discrimination Treatment based on class or race instead of individual merit.

epidemics Outbreaks of disease. They often spread quickly and affect a lot of people, especially if the people are living in crowded conditions.

exploited Used unfairly.

famine A time when food is very scarce because of weather or war.

ferment To change chemically.

immigrants People who leave one country to settle permanently in another.

imported To bring things in from another country.

industrialized Related to industry or the production of goods.

interest A charge for a loan, usually a percent of the amount loaned.

internment camps Places where people are sent during wartime if they are suspected of working with the enemy.

interpreter One who translates from one language to another.

justice Judge.

liberated Set free

lice Wingless biting insects.

Mafia A secret organization that was first set up in Sicily (an island off the coast of southern Italy). It became a criminal organization and was brought to North America in the nineteenth century by Italian immigrants.

patron saint A saint who reportedly protects or supports a city or an occupation.

prosperity Success.

quarry Places where rocks are dug out of the earth.

Index

1 2 3 4 5 6 7 8 9 0 Printed in the USA 5 4 3 2 1 0